I Believe

Written by Jamie Goldring
Illustrated by Katie Jones
Edited by Charlotte Zehring

ISBN: 978-1973718420

I believe in
MYSELF!

I believe in the passion
of a shooting star.

I believe in fairy tales, wishes, and magnificent feats.

I believe in trying as hard as I can, over and over and over again.

Encouragement and help are important to all.

I believe in
strength and
courage and in
peace and hope.

After reading *I Believe*, discuss the following questions.

(1) What is friendship? Name some things you can do to be a good friend.

(2) What are strength and courage? Name some different ways that you show strength and courage.

(3) What is sharing? Why is sharing important?

(4) What does it mean to trust yourself or to trust someone else?

(5) Name some things that make you feel good about yourself.

(6) Name some different ways you can help people whom you don't know.

(7) What does this sentence mean to you? *I believe in the beauty that shines from within.*

(8) What is knowledge? How can knowledge help your dreams come true?

(9) Name some different ways you can learn new things.

(10) What does this sentence mean to you? *I believe in myself!*

* Movement Activity

Teach children the following lines and movements to act out.

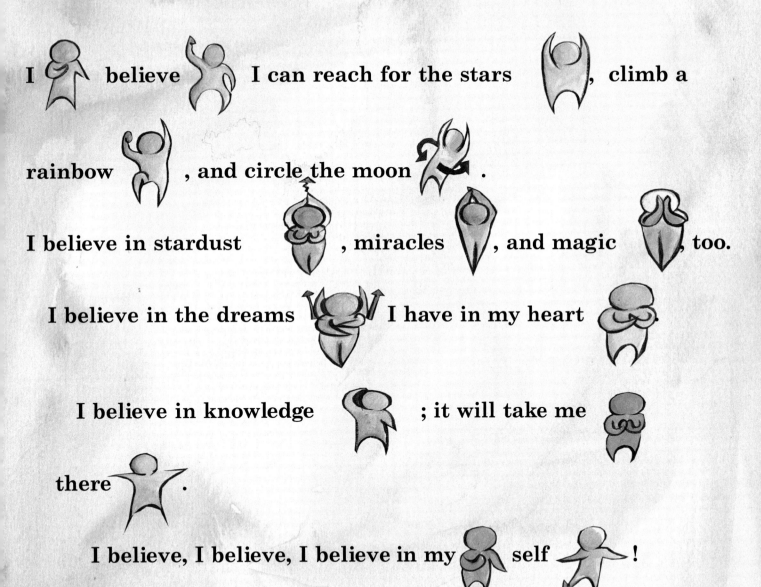

I believe I can reach for the stars , climb a

rainbow , and circle the moon .

I believe in stardust , miracles , and magic , too.

I believe in the dreams I have in my heart

I believe in knowledge ; it will take me

there .

I believe, I believe, I believe in my self !

*Refer to the movement explanations on the following page.

*Explanations to Clarify Movements

* I Believe - Repeat the "I believe" movement each time you say the words, "I believe."

* I - Point to yourself.

* Believe - Reach up high with your hand and pretend to pull the "belief" all the way down, bending your knees and placing your other hand on your leg, and say "believe."

* Stardust - Place your hands together in front of your body. Your palms should be touching and your fingers pointing up. Move your hands upward in a figure eight or a zigzagging pattern.

* Miracles - Stretch your arms and hands straight up above your head. Quickly criss-cross your hands back and forth twice (one hand in front of the other, and then change).

* Magic - Your hands should be covering your face but not touching it. Separate your hands. Snap your fingers one time. Clap your hands one time.

* Dreams - Quickly circle your hands around and around each other as they move upward. Stretch your arms straight up, hands open wide, and reach for your dreams.

* Me - Point to yourself with your thumbs.

Jamie Goldring has been working with children for more than thirty years. She specializes in teaching children self-control. Ms. Goldring is the author of Discover ME, Teaching Children Self-Control, and Tools and Techniques for Teaching Children Self-Control. She is also the creator of Color Your Way to Peace, Calm, and Tranquility, an interactive coloring book that teaches you how to calm your body and mind through self-awareness.

To learn more about teaching children self-control please visit www.teachingselfcontrol.com or email Jgoldie721@aol.com

Always Believe in Yourself,
The Dream Believer!